The Meaning of My Story:

By: Marshay Herder

Updated 1st Edition 2017

"**All rights are reserved to the publisher, author and owner of this book Marshay Herder**" **(Marshay Models Entertainment)**

No part of this publication may be reproduced, distributed, or transmitted in any form or by any means, including photocopying, recording, or other electronic or mechanical methods, without the prior written permission of the publisher, except in the case of brief quotations embodied in critical reviews and certain other noncommercial uses permitted by copyright law.

Index:

1. Keep Coming Back for More

2. Lost in Love

3. Stepping Zone

4. Bittersweet

5. Clean my Dirty Assets

6. Baby Born Not Alive

7. Religion vs. Religious

8. Same Me

9. Family Time and Empire

10. Distinction

11. Jayde

12. Jayde Part 2

13. Grandma (Yolande Gary)

14. Lost and Abandoned

15. USE

16. Split Faith

17. It Doesn't Exist

18. Transformers

19. There's A Calling over Your Life

20. Open Your Eyes

21. Destiny Lies

22. So Over

23. Once Upon A Time

24. Twinkle, Twinkle Little Star

25. Stole

26. Give Me Three Good Reasons

27. Baby Genius

28. Star

29. Borderline

30. Evolutions

31. Program

32. Added Sum

33. Play list

34. Watch

35. Isolation

36. Harmless

37. Mind

38. Another

39. My Love is Yours

40. You were and I was

41. Never Say Never

42, PIG

43, Everyone Knows

44, Next

45. Biblical Faith

46. No better

47. Food Bank

48. Happiness

49. Lopsided

50. Leave

51. Eye Popping Puzzles

52. True Baddest Chick

53. Ant

54. Couldn't Die

55. Picasso

56. Trapped In the Closet

57. Territory

58. City

59. Wild Child

60. Step Child

62. Dead

62. Castings

63. Against All Odds

64. Sunoco

65. Worst

66. False Prophecy

67. Prepared

68. Lives Here

69. Mood Change

70. Heart Definition

71. Pink or Blue?

72. BET

73. Pregnant with a Spiritual Birth

74. Hard Living Life

75. Sorry to Impose

76. #BlackBoys

77. Like Jesus is to god

78. Precious

79. Call

80. Forget that Fast

81. Play-DOH

82. I Do

83. My Choice

84. Left Eye

85. You were not here but there

86. My Awardee

87. Peace

88. There was no ending to the drama

89. No trespassing!

90. Wanting to do more than you can

91. My Frenemies

92. Tax Money

93. Forgiveness

94. Great Grandma Claudette

95. Rainbow

96. Light As A Feather

97. That Thing, That Thang

98. Three Blind Mice

99. Living On the Verge

100. Living On the Verge

1. What Does My Story Mean??

Why are you so quiet? What's wrong with you?

Why do you act like that? Why won't you play with us?

You're weird!! You're too quiet!! You're so shy!! You're crazy!! You act old!! Stop acting like that!!

Something's wrong with you….

Imagine being only eight years old and these are the words already etched in your head. The little girl in me never felt validated for her negative experiences but often felt the blame for what she experienced. The entire time people were asking me questions; I was questioning myself and the way I did that was on paper in poetic form. I wrote about the six-year old who was molested, the eight-year old who wanted her parents, the nine-year old who was told she sound like JaRule, the twelve-year old who was mocked in the hallway by two boys, and the fourteen year old fighting to get out of her pit of depression and the twenty year old hungry for success. The twenty-year old who finally had the confidence to release what she had been writing for years and instead of receiving hugs and love, her feelings were rejected. I almost went back to the girl who couldn't find the strength to continue but I was constantly reminded why I am writing and releasing my books. There is a young girl out there who is just like me, shy, quiet, and often reserved who has the passion to change the world but the fear of a cowardly lion. I fought for years to get out of this pit that I'd fallen in, eventually realizing that everything I've experienced was necessary for me to grow into the beautiful, smart and successful young woman I am, never have I been perfect and I never will be but I'm constantly striving to be my very best.

"The Meaning of My Story" 12 Modules

1. Knowing Your Worth (Poems 1-15)

2. Making Decisions and Choices (Poem 16-20)

3. Blood is Thicker (Poems 21-33)

4. Bounded By The Past (Poems 34-40)

5. Set Me Free (Poems 41-50)

6. I am My Sister (Poems 51-58)

7. Childlike Tales (Poems 57-67)

8. Worst Behavior (Poems 68-79)

9. Inside of Me (Poems 80-89)

10. My Heart Cry (Poems 90-97)

11. Never Ending (Poems 98-113)

12. I Envision (Poems 113-120)

Module 1: Knowing your Worth

In life, you will constantly search to be loved, appreciated and accepted while being neglected, devalued and diminished. It is up to you to determine your value and the way others will view your worth. There is no one on Earth who could replace you because the traits you carry are unlike no other, that is why God created you. God used your two parents to form you and he has plans for your life that no on Earth can cancel but it is your responsibility to carry out. Live this one life to the best of your ability as authentically and beautiful as you can. Problems will always come but who you are when no one is looking is the true test of character. This character and morality you carry out through your trials will show up after the battle is won. Do you like how I said "WON" because I already know you are a winner and winning. As special as you are, you have to be attacked in order to grow, you will lose yourself in order to learn yourself. It will all be worth it in the end.

We find out just how courageous we are when we face our ultimate fears. There was once a time where I questioned myself, now I question others, I stand firmly in who I am and the decisions I make. Remember to love you because I'd promise you my last dollar, God does.

Keep Coming Back For More

Keep Coming Back for More
Keep Coming Back for More

Every time I walk through the door

The energy reminds me
That something isn't right
But I keep walking in anyway
Expecting things to be different this time

Is a little foolish I know but when I'm gone, something feels different and it's not a bad feeling
But afraid that it will end up like my resting place, I leave after a short stay

Never wanting my stay to no longer be welcomed
She looks at other relationships and has the nerve to comment but is ours any better
No comment

We argue, fuss, almost every week, end up not speaking
For some reason, God is saying
This isn't supposed to be-------But how can it change?
If I'm only changing me
Our relationship is valued at if I'm willing to do what you ask
But as soon as I say No
That's it, time for you to go
The mistakes of my father
Your feelings they still harbor
Hard to truly be set free
When your control of my mind still binds me

And you may wonder how
And think my age has anything to do with it
But it has everything to do with your title, position and place and honestly

Sometimes I enjoy coming back for me
So, I'll just keep coming back for more

Lost in Love

I saw pass your looks that were never GQ
I loved you for you
Twisted in the head
Crazy you had problems but as your woman, I didn't care
I just wanted you there
Alcohol was your favorite beverage and your music career needed some leverage
I was willing to do anything for you to be mine
You came in the house late one night, drunk as always
You laid beside me and I felt your hand touch my hip
But I rolled over because you were probably with some other trick
You turn to me and ask why you act this way
I explain and you say
You haven't done a thing; this is the same ole' song you sing
Sick of hearing the excuses, like I don't know the misuses
I stress almost every day
Worried about where you stay
As we argue, I slip out and say
Yeah, I called your girl the other day
You ask, what did she say?
Well, she told me everything about you two and everything you do
You tried to play me as a fool
But this is the last day, See, I am no longer desperate for your attention and lust
I'm a woman, therefore, I must
Refuse to be treated this way, for I must understand the position I play
In business, I stand so strong, I fall to a level unlike me, thinking my expectations are far too grand
This relationship has gotten out of hand

I was on my way to being your wife but you live a double life, making everything seem like it's okay
When you know, our relationship struggles everyday
And there is no way, that I will continue to be
A weak ole' woman complaining you did this to me

Cause' now it's clear to see
I left my life in your hands and forgot about ME

Stepping Zone

I still fall on my face sometimes and I can't color inside the lines

I'm perfectly incomplete, I'm still working on my masterpiece!!

How can you give me a blueprint when you haven't even stepped in this field?

You can't tell me what you would've when you haven't taken that risk

You've always stuck to what you know and I'm not blaming know, it's comfortable and safe

But my spirit and mindset tells me to do otherwise and being around others who don't push me in some form holds me back

It's not your fault, it's mines, I am just my own kind

I am not comfortable living this way and with no guidelines, well; what can I say

The road hasn't been set and the pavement isn't wet but yet I still feel, feel an urge to be different than those around me

They call me crazy and I'll agree, I step out of boundaries that were never set there for me and dare to be!!

What they could never see, but I'll keep trying because that way

I'll never fail and my life will be in heaven, not spent in hell

I'm God's child, I will prevail

Nothing wrong with doing right, don't let others stop your fight

Struggle, and you'll be alright, live life how you believe God wants you to and the rest he takes care of for you

Mistakes are okay and will be made along the way, worth every day you kneel

With your head bowed and your hands mashed together, often tears on your face

One thing God offers you during this difficult space

His Grace!!

Bittersweet

One day it's Monday and I think were so in love

Then comes Tuesday and he puts his other priorities above

So, I call Wednesday, and we make love

Then Thursday comes and he buys me dinner

Friday, I go to out to eat and Saturday comes early to meet me

Sunday, I relax and go to church

This is just as hard as work

My week is "Bittersweet"

Oh, so bittersweet

Clean My Dirty Assets

Soap and water all over my body
Wishing I could wash away the scum from somebody
No, Not just him
That somebody is me
I know that may not be what you see
But the truth lies inside of me
Ferociously
I get angry just thinking about what I've done
After All, God gave his only son
But for what?? For me to feel
Feel, fill this void that lingers around
Making me feel like I should drown
I remember as a child, all the kids would be outside swimming in the pool
I was inside, looking through the window
But for who
You, yea, you Mama
And I didn't have to look too far
because I'd point and say there you are
You were always across the street
Hands on your knees and your butt in the air
Twerking was invented by you but don't nobody care
Miley didn't have nothing on you besides her amount of cash
Mama, you were so pretty
And every man that ever knew you, wanted to be with you
People told me I look like you but that

I could never do
I am light with messy freckles on my face
And short and small, I'm always out of place
But that's beside the point, I walk around with so much shame
It's not a game, I hate it when it's done
But I do it every day so it must be fun
I go see Mike and he pays me in cash
But wait, it's never good money when a transaction is made that fast
So, I say what's up? Mike, I know this isn't for what I normally do
He says I will never ask more out of you
I look at him and I laugh
We enter the abandoned building
And we enter this room
It's empty and wide and it already has a bed inside
Mike lays down and then so do, I
As I get on top of him, someone comes behind me
Jokingly, I laugh
Thinking its Mike who couldn't keep his hands to himself
Until I realize, Mike's hands are around my neck
I try to turn around and get up but Mike's grip is way too tight
I say to Mike, what's going on?
He says just do your job and be quiet
As his friend, no longer just had his hands on my butt
But he has entered his privates in me
Ready to Truck
I try to scream but I realize no sound is coming out
My mouth is covered with two large hands, and they aren't Mike's or his other friend
This guy begins to do something that I can't even write and at this point, I begin to fight
But they are way too strong
Just like Nikko

His hands would hit Mama's face so hard, I'd be scared, thinking she isn't alive
He'd knock her out a couple of times and then come looking for me
But he'd sweet talk me and say
Come on, come play
If you want Mama to be okay
I've been dirty for so many years, I don't know what it's like to be clean
But it's about time, I get my dirty butt up
And put some Soap and Water All Over My Body
So, that's what I do, I get up, wash up and I get dressed
But I'm no longer wearing the same clothes and No, that's not because I think I'm better than anyone else
As some of my closest enemies would say
Clean My Dirty Assets

Baby Born but Not Alive

Could I survive if I had a baby born but not alive?

My head begins to spin as I see the photo, I believe God is

watching me but I'm not screaming YOLO

I just couldn't fathom what I would feel

Seeing the picture has made it real

Religion VS. Religious

Well Let Me Get this Straight
You believe in submission to a man but have you ever yet submitted to God?
You believe that God doesn't want man to be rich but have all his needs but all your life, you've searched for money in greed?
You believe you couldn't follow a preacher who doesn't have anything but you expect your child to follow you and you're not going anywhere?
You believe in Jesus you say, but your actions are far from God's way?
You said he says Pray, but are you praying for yourself?
We live in a world where it's easy for folks to state what they believe but have no reasoning or purpose behind those beliefs but they say God does things and you may not know how and why but know that it is God
So, I say God is the reason that you'll believe what you do because he's my reason
When I stand up for something that I believe is right, it's not because I need something to write
It's because his power, aligned me right
Everything doesn't need to be explained because God's plans are insane
Have you ever noticed that when one area of your life increased, problems arisen in other areas of your life?
That is the Devil trying to interrupt God's plan for you but if you become focused only on God's promise, the Devil becomes afraid and you begin to succeed in all areas of life
Devils chase those who are doing God's work
Remember, the key to opening the gates to heaven is work
But the joy that awaits is worth all the wait

Same ME

You want everything to be back to normal to feel the same
but your ideas of me still haven't changed
I'm supposed to just lay in bed
and feel alright when you're the same one who cussed me
out that night
I'm sorry but I'm extra sensitive and I just can't get over it,
that fast
I wanted our bond to last but who you think I am
I don't know her and I keep digging trying to see, if there's
just a small percentage of me
that feels like that girl that would do something so cruel
I just drop tears and I drool
Over the fact that you believe that's who I am
I can't prove you otherwise
Who I am in Gods eyes
I pray that you learn to admit and adjust
Just sit down and discuss
Why I choose not to stay at your house anymore
and I can't say I'm not hurt
because I've always been

I'm just realizing that I NEED A FRIEND

I NEED A FRIEND

I NEED A FRIEND

this is not the same ME

Family Time

It's time to party, it's time to have fun

Get Up Every one!! Everyone!!!!

I see my aunties, cousins are on their way

And I'm feeling like life couldn't be better today

I'm just happy, we all the chance to celebrate

Appreciate your family, I hope they appreciate you, too

Happiness, Laughter and Love is what we need to do

{It's family time, start to do what your family needs you to do}

{They'll be there for you< Family Time!!}

{Family, play with me-We'll live life happily}

Dance, sing, play games, and everything you love to do

Enjoy your life, it's up to u

Thank you, Jesus!!

Empire

From the ground up

An Empire was built

Not off excuses and mixed with a little guilt

Past mistakes led to the future trials

Situations causing family disruptions, lasting awhile

Distinction

Been together for a long time

Now I think it's time for me to write a song
How long can you sit and be around me?

knowing we aren't never get nowhere
We reached our highest and were already there
So, stop sleeping with me every night

I don't know how I made it through every fight
but God something isn't right
Ain't I'm supposed to be a wife

I sometimes think when you're there, things feel better
but that's my mind playing tricks and I keep on letting her
God, I need you to tell me the truth

I want my business to grow but I'm personally not listening to you—So

God, let me know
The difference in your face and the devils, it should show
Help Me grow!!

Can't keep on sinning in God's world, doing what I want when I'm God's girl

There's a certain distinction between me and you
I can't continue to do what you do
This is not made for me but created for me

No more talking, let me show you what I'll do

Jayde

My favorite person in the world
My favorite little girl
I will miss your smile and the way you talk
Of course, I'll miss those duck feet and the way you walk
I'll miss your cry and I'll miss when you say No
It's hard for me to imagine never saying Hello
I'll miss you saying Soda Good and telling me what to do
I'll miss Peppa Pig almost as much I miss you
I'll miss the way you pointed to my shoulder
Anyone who knows Jayde, knows this is how she loves for you to hold her
I'll miss taking you to dance practice with Miyah and Bri
I'll miss you ever getting the chance again to ride with me
Your parents have been strong and stuck by your side, everyday
God couldn't have blessed you in a better way
I'll miss seeing you dance and laugh your way through life
I'll miss my best friend, I've ever had in my life
I know that you now are healed
By God's stripes, I'm so thankful
But I cannot pretend like my heart doesn't wish that you are still here
For me to hold and kiss - For me to come and see
Thank God that he chose you
To be so special to just bless the world for two
Two years you have been here and already so many lives you've changed
Just imagine when your gone, your legacy will do the same
This I promise you Jayde is not the end
I love you forever, until we meet again

Grandma (Yolande Gary)

Grandma, out of everyone I knew
You were the most like me
Strong and stubborn as can be
You put your kids first
And provided everything that they would need
There for your grand kids, too and there is never enough in the world we could do
To show you how much we appreciate you

Especially me, you would never fall for what others would say
Even when they called me crazy
You weren't throwing dirt on my name
But instead you always welcomed me with a smile
And even asked "are you staying for a while?"
You would give without me asking for a thing

Feed me, and allow me to grow
Right in your very house and I've never been one to not appreciate what you do
Without you grandma, what is there for me to hold on to?
You watch American Idol, which you knew I loved and asked me who I wanted to stay?
And I'd scream when they went away
You call me randomly just to check up on me and see how I feel
You were my place I could always run to, my shield
We didn't argue or fight, and I'm not saying, we did everything right
But our birthdays were a week apart
And you are one of the sentiments to my heart
A Taurus, we both are!!

No one understands the way that you protect your card or purse

But I understand just that feeling, it's nothing we could coerce

On anyone else, it is our thing that only we would understand, we keep the things we care about close to us

Afraid to let it go, and your baby Jayde

I understand how that felt to see her lay in a casket and not be able to reach out her arms
And say grandma
You could never get back that feeling and it truly hurts
Losing your sister shortly before was something I could not put in to words
Dealing with this every day, everybody you love, just dying away
And you've raised your kids the best you could and I have to say, you've done pretty good
All of us have traits of you
My mother has your lips and nay wears the same hairstyle as you
And pooh, looks almost exactly like you
I carry your stubbornness and your stand your ground attitude
Keami has your burp, and as gross as this may sound, it's true

We're all little snippets of you

Jalan is cool and laid back

Bri is your wilder side and remember, when you use to put your one leg up

You passed your dancing on to Miyah, and now she could never get enough

Landon bites his tongue but he doesn't yet count to ten and Jayde, even though her life did end

She loved you beyond imagine

She is your heart, we all are

And if you didn't know before, you are ours

Everything about you, I admire and pray that one day I'm able to help as many as you have

And do it with grace, you're truly blessed if they've never told you before

We love you ever more!!!

Lost and Abandoned

This title fits what I'm about to write
For I have a fit, I began to type
This feeling has come in my life so often
I'm afraid it will never go
But I promise God, I'll let Go
No one around me quite understands
The way I feel God carries me in his hands
I thought I understood his plan
But to be entrapped in a lost State -Feeling like I'm unable to climb this gate
Has caused me to feel like a child being raped
Screaming and hollering on the inside that one day I'll be able to do on my own
What people have passed along
I never had parents to depend on, and at times that makes me sad
Having this neglected feeling, being angry like my dad
I know that I have dreams, goals and plans but they take required work that I'm willing to do
But as a human being, there is nothing I can do alone
And having no one to help me has caused me to keep singing the same song
Dear Mama, I would understand you not having if you didn't give so freely to others
And be there for others to use, to borrow from and to need
But for your own child, you don't understand my needs
You neglect me, honestly and I have never done the same to you
Most kids in my case, would've hated you but I don't
Most kids in my case, would disrespect you but I won't
Most kids in my case, would get in so much trouble that you
become in trouble but I can't

Instead, I carry myself as God has taught me and I love you despite everything you have and have not done

You wonder why I'm upset, who to this day do you call when you need help, and can lean on

Your Mother
Yes, Your Mother
But for me, I can't say the same
But I'm too old to even play this same game and blame things in my life on you
Nope, it's my fault, too- I can admit my wrongs

Allowing people to treat me wrong
Doing for others and not wanting nothing in return
Working hard for everything I earned

But now, I know, I do for those who are willing to do for themselves because everyone else are in the circumstances they are in, for a reason and therefore I won't give any excuses anymore
I'll just say "God use me and open up the door"

☐ Lost and abandoned no more

USE

People will use you until you can't be used anymore
Abuse you until you can't be abused no more
All for what they need
Then when it comes down to your needs
They could simply care less
but you know what's so funny
I was the only one there to help you
And I guess that's why nobody else was willing to help you
People are so much smarter than you think
They know your heart and this isn't the first time somebody has felt this way
You call, I'm there
I'm suffering and you run away
But the great thing about Marshay is I never stay down for long
I'm what they call- Super Strong
I always find the strength to get up and make a way
No way I'm going to struggle everyday
When they think it's the end, it's just a second beginning
So Glad, I'm smarter now, won't make the same mistake twice
Next time I won't throw my heart away
words of advice from Keyshia Cole
I'm sensitive, this I know
People Listen Up
Don't, I repeat
Do NOT
Bend over backwards for anybody that doesn't deserve it
The only people I could think of, that's deserving are your kids

Anybody who helps you that is who you help, and those who can help themselves
Extend an Olive Branch and those who takes a interest in your soul and not your physical being or your physical use
You are not worth what you can do for others
Your value is far beyond intimate lovers

Warning: Anytime somebody ask what you doing?

They don't really care; they just want to know what you're willing to do for them!!

Remember:

When they ask what, you are doing, say working for the Lord, that will surely throw them off!!

Split Faith

"Strength where I've been weakened, Forever, he will reign" (Song)
God, I please ask you to teach me the way
Seems like my instructor has gone astray
I can't be directed by someone with split faith
When I proclaim to be filled with God's Grace
They scream, holler and shout Hallelujah
But you pay attention to the things they do to ya'
"I agree but I don't, I will but I won't"
That's how they sound, can't keep switching around
Black and White, filled with stripes
Like segregation in race, it ain't right
This is what causes fights; I'm cheating but I don't want you to
That's the kind of things, I do
I'll say "where have you been?"
But ask a question and I'll defend
I say "Why you eating that?"
But I'm the one who is getting fat
I say "Who is that?"
And I tell you that you shouldn't
But I'm just saying that because I couldn't
"Strength where I've been weakened, Forever, he will reign"
God, this is my domain
Guide me as I move each day
Protect me in every way
Lead me down the path that you choose
Direct me and I'll never lose
But when I break, you'll hold on tight and in the end of the night, it will be alright

Module 2: Making Decisions and Choices

You will be faced with some of the hardest decisions in your life when you are closest to reaching your destiny. All hell is going to break loose, remain steadfast in who you are, choose GOOD even when Good seems not to be choosing you. Make the decision to choose LOVE over FEAR, love will keep you moving, fear will hold you back. God has a placed those around you for a reason, understand their purpose in your life and allow them to serve just that. Sometimes the thing that you'll love most, you'll have to let go. Hold onto your faith and don't be afraid to discover facets life has to offer to life. The decision to be the best version of yourself is the best choice you could ever make even if it means to rid yourself of something you've done for years.

Old habits and mindsets can be broken but it will take time, work and focus. Focus on being WHOLE alone and of course, enjoying the company of others. Accept you and honor you when no one is around. Choose to value your roots and where you come from, it is tied to your future.

It Doesn't Exist

She'd still stay forever, said I'll always be your friend
The bruises on my neck, there's no way the abuse will end

But in front of my family, I will pretend
It's best if I see them only when I need

My love to him was like a disease
It had me going to the lord, praying on my knees
His attitude is demanding, filled with greed
Money was the only thing to him that could please

I did everything I could to please him
Why Stay, you may ask, he gives me love
Sort of like a dad, Something I've never had

At times, he's fun and hilarious, too
I would've never agreed if he didn't give me something I need
No one would provide for me and protect me in this way
What else could I say?

It Doesn't Exist

Transformers

You were my Jada, I was your Tupac
Suddenly, our relationship stopped

You no longer called me every day
You pushed me away
But as always I would stay
I guess your boo been good to you, today

So now you're ready to travel

Go along for the ride

And I'm supposed to just sit here
Stand by your side

Transformer not a reformer
But he's your former, and you're a performer

Don't wonder why things go the way they do
Your joy is temporary, sooner than later he will leave you

Then bitter, you'll be crying
Sour, told you he was lying

Sweet, he could be
There's deception and manipulation, I guess you couldn't see
Transformers have that ability

They know exactly how and when to change
Their victims are all the same

There's a calling over your life

This was declared by your wife
She was so calm and peaceful, even though you did something so evil
I was frightened because I know that once you lose your mind, it's lost until you gain it back through mankind
Afterward you thought "You were wrong"
But who am I to believe you, when I've heard ya' sing that same song, went to the extent of saying you're going to kill ya' self, but the calling over your life, declared otherwise
Therefore, I'm similar to you but we are not the same
I don't play those games
I called you names that day that you'd thought you'd never hear from Shay
The pain you left me with, did not just walk away
I'd had sleepless nights of thoughts that weren't alright
Wasn't trying to display you as a monster cause within every monster, lies an angel whose wings were clipped, who've lost their strength-When I think about you, I'm no longer angry, I drop a few tears, just wishing you were here
We've had moments that I've never had with anyone else, you made me like the worst as a child
Like no love was allowed
But then there were those times when no one else was around, and I felt like you bowed down and gave me your crown
The man who's supposed to make me feel protected, made me afraid to sleep
For days, I couldn't sleep on my own, then I couldn't shut my door
I was experiencing what you once had
I figured out what caused you to be sad

You had expectations that others' love couldn't reach
and your definition of Love, they surely didn't teach
You once had high hopes for us all wishing that they'd fill your heart
Every single part
But they didn't meet that bar, didn't recognize you were a star
You fell into a depressive state, mental state so steep
All you could do was weep
You continued with your charades but deep down, you're afraid
You aren't quite sure what to expect
And your child don't forget, you did Neglect

BUT YOU'RE SO MUCH BETTER THAN THIS

Open Your EYES

How you neglect me emotionally

You never really knew how I felt

You told me to put on my lipstick and act grown

Your true immaturity was shown

You think u are Nene on Atlanta housewives

You've reached the top but baby, I'm going to have to tell you

The gifts will stop if you keep pretending to be someone you are not

Depending on the place, the spot

Module 3: Blood is Thicker

"Blood is thicker than water" is a statement often heard but not quite, lived by. I am suggesting that through reading these poems you'll be able to determine who is there for you, what their intentions are and how you should treat everyone accordingly. Family is vital, having people who genuinely care, support and want the best for you is something out of this world GOOD, live in LOVE, choose people who encourage you, uplift, laugh with you and correct you. Look for friends who don't just agree with you but challenge to grow and be the best that you could be. Water is loose and fluid while blood is thick and dense, stronger and more fluid. Choose people who will care for you when you have made mistakes, choices that are good and bad, who will love you in your mess. They are your "Ohana" and Ohana means "family."

Friends are great to have, people who support your decisions and value you. If the people around you throw dirt on your name, taint you, and/or devalue your worth, rid your life of them after discussing how they have hurt your feelings and how you can improve. They should care about how you feel, what they say and how it has affected you. Your roots create branches that branch out but often remains intact too its tree, don't allow where you are from to determine where you are going.

Destiny Lies

Where does your destiny lie?
Everyone wants to know but no one wants
to discover
Afraid that their deepest secrets will
uncover

How they are like NO OTHER

But that is a lonely road that no one
wants to travel
Over the road bumps and gravel
The pathway is gradual
But the results will leave you baffled

Distraught and baffled you once were
You are no longer in a blur
But instead look within yourself

And find what brings you joy
Know God has a plan for you
And begin to Enjoy!!

Your Destiny Lies in God's Eyes

So Over

We are often reflections of our parents

Experiencing the same relationship difficulties of our

mothers

With our father's ego's- Close to each other

We see what they go through and we hate what we see

But no matter how much we deny it, it becomes a part of

me

We lie about the similarities we share and we pretend we

don't even care

At times, our lives are so much fun

We get excited when a NEW Day has begun

I'm So Over being afraid to care because no one has ever

truly been there

I'm So Over being depressed because I no longer can live

life stressed

I'm So Over being broke because my finances are not a

joke

I'm So Over being helpless and tired

I'm re-energized with a new faith

I just Got Hired

So Over, So, Over, So Over, SO OVER

Once Upon A TIME

I've never been awakened by a kiss

I've always been struggling with this

This fear to speak, like Cinderella, I feel weak

There's Beauty to speaking up but I'm too afraid of the Beast

Like Tiana, I have dreams but to come to reality is difficult it seems

My Beast is like Mermaid's father

Expecting me to stay within its boundaries and never go any farther

Writing is my Aladdin

It takes me on a journey like Jasmine

After I finish, I'm gasping

All of a sudden, I'm laughing

Like Rapunzel, my hair is blond

But I don't speak to animals like Pocahontas

My feelings have always been in a harness

but I consider myself honest

The Devils wishing for my Death like Aurora

(uh-Roor-a)

But I'll fight back like Mulan, I'll be the Scorer

Twinkle, Twinkle Little Star

Twinkle, Twinkle Little Star

Now, I wonder how you are
When I look at your old photos, I see the sparkle in your eye but for some reason, you let your sparkle die

I used to ask God why
Do all your chosen ones die?

at such a young age, my spirit was filled with rage
I now realize what drove me insane
For so long, I've hid my pain
I never wanted to be a sob story

But it comes everywhere I go
I let it affect me, you know

At 6 or 7, I remember things that happened to me
That same thing haunts me to this day before I sleep
Now I'm yelling, I see a creep

Twinkle, Twinkle Little Star
Like your pregnant, you began to glow
Six months, let your big belly show

The development process, is amazing "Let Go"

Stole

Stole the faith you had in the Ultimate Man
Made you live according to his plan

The relationship you once had become sour
Now your heart, he's starting to devour

He thought man ruled the world
Deserved all the power

made you work for every dime
But you enjoyed every minute together, you loved to spend time

such a disharmonious environment
It was perfect for you -- the complications are what attracted you

he knew exactly what to do
profess his love to you

Then make you feel like you needed him
So, nice at times and often sweet, you thought

you found your soul mate

but really
U found Hell's Gate

Give Me Three Good Reasons

Didn't even want to hear about your long day
But everything somebody does, he has so much to say
As you talk, he walks away
But as a woman, you let him stay
Insulted a kid
He must be out of his mind
He must have never met my kind
I only take but so much for so long
1st step is me mentioning you in my song
Then u call me dirty cause I did you wrong
Act like u was a victim, all along

Number 1: You Lie

Number 2: Who are you?

Number 3: Not my Fam-i-ly

Baby Genius

Kids are the greatest humans to exist

They are fearless when they complete a task like this

Filled with many talents and gifts

We often wait until they make a mistake

Then it's too late, to obligate

They take everything in-And are true to their friends

Respectful and often kind, the hate they gain over time

Different- each one of them are------ The difference creates a Star

At 5, teach em' to drive a car

It multiplies the brain cells they've developed so far

On the playground with jump ropes and hula hoops, they created a castle

Their work skills were no hassle, A story she could tell over in a unique way

Gia is a writer, what else can I say?

Except Children are the greatest gifts TODAY

Star

Shining
Through
All
Rain

The sky is the limit, no that is just the view
You are the passport and the crew

Life's possibilities are up to you

When I see passion
You are life's living proof

You never mind telling the truth
So, good at everything you do
Sounds like I'm falling in Love with you

Confidently, you gently
Have such a gift
When performed, today's task has a lift

You sparkle and your glow
The feeling you give, only I know

People say I'm obsessed and I sometimes feel that way
because your Light
It never goes away
You Make Me Everyday

Borderline

The edge of a cliff-I'm on

My emotions have been torn

Crazy, no longer describes me, I'm insane
My job is not what drains

But my intuitive thoughts and my inside desires

Has my soul burning on fire
One thing I never am
A liar

I've been called weird by half the world
I want to help them imperiled

The edge of a cliff-I'm on
When I look down, I see the chaos in the world and I almost fall into it

But I'm Marshay, I couldn't do it

Evolution's

" EVOLUTION IS ANY CHANGE ACROSS SUCCESSIVE GENERATIONS IN THE INHERITED CHARACTERISTICS OF BIOLOGICAL POPULATIONS"

We come into the world, searching for One Thing

We come into our teenage years, searching for One Thing

We come into our midlife crisis, searching for One Thing

We come into our senior citizens ages, searching for

One Thing

WE LIVE AND DIE FOR ONE THING

THAT THING IS LOVE so

HAVE WE EVOLVED?

NO, BECAUSE THE PROBLEM IS STILL NOT SOLVED

Program

The program that you set up, keep pushing me back while
I'm trying to move Forward

Now, I'm looking like you whack and I'm starting to ignore it

But sometimes the skills of it, I adore it

Set to ring at an early time
Ding, Ding, ding that's all that's on my mind

My life, I need to align
Younger entrepreneurs everyday

Time to press Play
Get started Today
Sick of living life this way

Underachiever with So MUCH TO SAY

I GOTTA GET READY FOR JUDGEMENT DAY

Added Sum

I lift you up and I Love you More

I am the Added Sum

Unexpected arrival, I made
Ever since that day, you wouldn't trade
Nothing in the world for a spade

Your him, he and her lied in ME

My 2 + your 4 equaled 6

Just like a CUBE with 4 sides and 2 times as much as this
I write it but I quite don't know what it means to me but
one day " I WILL"

Been There, Done That

Often we hear- Been there, done that
but have you really?
Have you ever walked a mile in my shoes?
I mean really?

We may wear the same size
And even our lives appear the same
But my inner me
Is my biggest enemy that you could never be
And I know you want to help
But maybe that's not what I need

What I have to offer?
You think you can lead
But this path is unusual and only for me
Something God planned perfectly and each step, I don't know but I'm willing to travel along the ride

Open up, let's see what's inside

Play-list

Played the song over and over

Same beat and rhythm

affected me the same way

Never trust that Lady

You knew ever since you were young

But still you make the same mistake

Come over just to be hurt
Nothing but Work
The first person on the list to be played is You
But this seems like it is what you LOVE to do

Module 4: Bounded By The Past

At the tender age of 14, my past had me bounded, I was emotionally chained and my physical body had become negatively numb to the things around it. At 21, I am fighting to regain my ability to FEEL because for years, I trained myself to ignore my feelings. The past had me thinking that hell would be my "Destiny" because of the pain I passed onto others because of the pain I was in. God snatched my wig and reminded me that the sad and solemn me had to die for Marshay to live. I decided that my future was far too grand to settle for my current state of allowing "what happened to me" to be "who I am:" when you allow your circumstance to overtake you, you are as bad as the intruder because you are constantly taunting yourself with what was instead of being so happy that people won't believe it was once your experience. Experiences shape you, it is okay to make mistakes and be imperfect, just learn what lesson has been taught in every experience.

Watch

I told you to pay close attention to what u do
You thought I was threatening you
But I was preparing you for the world
adventures and mistakes
Past the white snowflakes
I saw a Blue Sky, that Caught my eye cause
one day we'll wave it Hi

so I guaranteed I'd return there by doing all I
was supposed to while physically here
Next Time, don't cover your ear
Everywhere U go, you learn something new
There's always something to do
Just watch what I say
Just like the old, I don't the play
Your life can be changed today!!

Isolation

I so lonely here by myself
Left here with nothing but wealth
This is isolation at its best
where have you been when I was a mess
All you could was say God Bless
They say the top is lonely-
Got damn, I could have had at least one homey
I wasn't prepared for this
Thought I'd live in Simple Bliss
I'm feeling like F--K This
My money can't talk
My cars can't walk
The suitcase is bulk
I need Somebody
Looks like I'll have to Accompany
them Grudgingly

Harmless

When I gave you away
It was the last day

I've ever felt so wrong
But I felt it was right

That was my darkest-brightest night
You were beautiful to my site
I thought u would be alright

What child would want me as a parent?
Young, uneducated and broke
All I do is smoke

Time passed and I thought of you
But I thought there was nothing I could do
Till' I entered Rehab and there was you

My heart exited my chest as I fell for Cardiac Arrest
When that decision was made, I thought it was best
Harm-Less

but it turned out to harm you more
I've hurt you to the core, knowing that your mother had not
been your Mom

I swear, I didn't mean no harm

Mind

"Those who matter, don't mind
Those who mind, don't matter"

Your thoughts are yours, you choose to share
Handle them with Care
Beware

The world is filled with tricksters but remember Magic is
fake, so when the rabbit exits the hat

It's a mistake
Everything that you share is a risk, U Take

Think Before You do
Something that I individually would like to teach you

Think of him who guides your Life
Through your difficulties and strife
Intelligence comes with a high price

Don't have no Mindless Behavior
I'm trying to do you a Favor

Another

He treats u like u r just another
another one of his many

You are talked to like trash
told to "kiss his ass"

Slapped every single day that pasts
still the relationship lasts

he is in control of your every move
he knows everything that u do

I know he has your heart

and feel closer to the end then the start
But to me, you should Part

Go your separate ways and you will have
happier days

My Love is Yours

I know the love that you have
it's hidden behind your laugh
I know deep down you wish and you hope
just like the moment when you tell a joke
I know the reason you appear mean
your willpower isn't seen
I know that your misunderstood
but with that type of anointment, who could?
My love is Yours
it is not the price of the gift but the spirit that comes with
we both understand
but it's so hard to control the thoughts f man
get em' to follow God's plan
My Love is Yours
Whole and Complete
Loving and Deep
Different and Unique
Special and A Treat
Powerful and Never weak
If ever we could just get past the outside and look within
Within each other we'd find a Friend

You were and I was

U were a fighter for your dreams

a dignitary it may seem

I was a hopeful, a younger you

with so many visions beyond the sky that's Blue

You were overprotective and often strong

u had difficulties admitting you were wrong

I was feeling like I missed my opportunity

I was in need of immunity

U were still in pain

and I have to admit, I'm the Same

Module 5: Set Me Free

After discovering that the past is just that, THE PAST. You will discover that your old mindset must leave your body and a "new you" should takeover. You must be set free from what you imagined life would be. What people use to see you as should no longer exist but who you are is your MAIN FOCUS. You are constantly growing, and making decisions to be exactly who God created you to be. Feel free to express yourself in any manner (legal) you may choose. Be brave with your approach, realize that each day is a new day to do something new. Something new always brings about growth that you experience something that you haven't before.

This will bring about a newfound confidence and love for life. Having joy in life will cause a happiness that makes you want to stay up when you're supposed to be sleep. I let fear contain me for years, I don't want you to do the same thing. You don't have to continue to be bump on the log (no pun intended). Step out of that box of fear that you've been in for years. Sometimes life can be reckless, don't allow the wreck to make you fold but grab your dreams by the vision and handle your business.

Never Say Never

If I was to ever
look at the world in your eyes
I'd discover the cover of my secret demise

the sight of it causes my insides to cry
As a Christ lover, I can't lie
I've had moments that I won't deny
Things that I try

But why?

Ever feel so hopeless
With the problem u can't cope this
What will I do?

cause I'm still sitting here talking to u
the Paper instead of the People

Marshay, I can't believe U
I thought my miracle would be here by Now but I'm Still
searching around

But I will Never Say Never

PIG

Low down and dirty
you've been with every woman that looks sturdy
you didn't even care if she was pretty
had a wife at home with three kids

you didn't know how many others were yours because all their mothers were whores
tight tee and nice tennis shoes
she always did everything for you

6ft even and a nice body frame
the type of man, no woman could tame
I consider u lame

In need of what your wife provides so u won't leave her alone
you think u won the thrown

look at u, Mr. Big shot
Now good looks is all you've got

every girl you have been with is missing
now it's your wife's butt your sitting there kissing

her every wish is your command
you'd do anything to be her man

I demand you to think before u do
cause don't no woman want u

relax and accept it
it's a fact, u can't neglect it

Everyone knows

Your pain I feel it, your desire I wish I could kill it, Split it
The person whom we all Love, your spirit is that of a dove
But a drug enters your body
all of a sudden, you don't know nobody
Your no longer able to make letters, words
Your personality is curved
Your son is afraid I seen it in his eyes
Situation like Tupac, the day of my demise
God gave you an uncommon power, the place you are living is sour
your same friends that's what you call them
when u were in the Pen could u call them
Did they think of ways to help you or they left you
notice that only one person was there for you and he will always be close to you
but don't become a coaster to, your problems shouldn't bury you but carry you
Gods courage inherited you
Exposure **brings disclosure**
Eight years ago, at church
Pastor spoke of demons, too many men, you forgot whose semen
Mistakes folks will never get, like your club I.D., it was never legit
You and Your Mother Both were the Shit but Quit
Gods ultimate plan, i speak of
You could have been a leader like he does
Afraid to get out
like a mute kid who can't Shout
Yes, a father you were left without
Your pain, I don't doubt
It's Time to Get Out

drugs solve nothing, a little relaxation you feel
It keeps you a little mentally stable, your Ideal
What about his Will?
Would you risk it all for a thrill?
Choose this time period in your life to get real
Not Time to Stand Still
Things could quickly go downhill
At morning evening noon and Day
I'm Praying for You Please Get Away

Next

Ministries God Allow, Allow God's Ministries

Gods, the biggest liar's enemy

Believe what you did, he didn't defend himself

You can notice hi works through the miracles we've Overcome

Some just don't believe in his Son

God never says he's done'

He can fly you on a jet, in less than ten seconds he then done that

How A blind person begins to send?

Is how My Life Missions he sends to me

I join his Ministries

NEXT, the Unthinkable happens, I'm Rapping

Believe what you did, he didn't defend himself

You can notice hi works through the miracles we've Overcome

Some just don't believe in his Son

God never says he's done'

He can fly you on a jet, in less than ten seconds he then done that

How A blind person begins to send?

Is how My Life Missions he sends to me

I join his Ministries

NEXT, the Unthinkable happens, I'm Rapping

Biblical Faith

A woman with a hemorrhage problem, only one man could solve them
A crowd blocked her way

Bleeding, others thought it was her last day

But she pushed through with Faith
Till the moment she saw his face
Grabbed the bottom of his clothes, lace

against the devil, she won the race
Now God had to face: those that didn't know his face
even when he left a trace

He had healed, delivered and Set Free
But others thought he was ordinary like you and Me

The Faith of god you must carry, the fruit you must bury
To receive the fruit you are in a hurry
Don't Worry

You'll receive a Cherry(Cheer)

No Better

Talked about how she didn't do this and all she'd do was that but look at yourself

What do you do?

Talk behind her back, speak of how she'd lack and how "that's so wrong"

Think of all the moments I've sung the same song
You are No Better, your situation is No Better, you're not making the situation No Better

so, you mine as well let her, she'll learn one day and so will you
"I'll make up to you" that I constantly heard

It was missing one important word, Love (you)

For some reason, you thought I was fulfilled, I felt your love was on left field

I was on the right
Had me crying for a minute at night

No Better, I'd be lying if I write

You Were

Food Bank

Give back to those who are in need, not to those filled with greed

Poverty deserves a headline on the paper, not disgraceful, "I'll see you later"

If it was you, your expectations would be high

But show em' a life to wave the drugs Goodbye

Teach em' how to be a man so in life he could get by

Not the liquor is his priority to buy

Just Try

If you don't succeed, it's on them

At least you'll help Those in Need

A blessing to the ministry indeed

Food Bank, Fill the Food Tank

Happiness

Success is Happiness
Love is Happiness
God is Happiness
Strive for it and Keep it

Lopsided

Contradiction, Confliction
Not always what you think
The biggest preacher could be a skank
The best gangster rapper, you wouldn't think
Always wearing a tank and carrying a drank
Respectable and smarter than half of you
The image you see is only halfway True
The lopsided view of you
With your strong presence they wouldn't know what to do
Appears boring but get close to her and you won't have no time for snoring
You say she's always whoring but the moment she covers up, your ignoring'
A freak you say they've formed but true confidence is a rare form
Out of the norm

Leave

The moment you come is the moment I want you to leave

If you were smart, u would give me that relief

Cause the happiness, I had you pushed it away

Who asked you to ruin my day

How come alone I find so much peace?

Around you I leave in grief

Module 6: I am My Sister

As Iyanla taught us all through her women's healing house, I am not my sisters keeper, I am my sister. This statement simply means that I am not just there for my sister and her journey, but despite what I know, our journeys are one in the same. My experiences are very similar to my sisters without us every acknowledging. We may point our fingers and speak about our sisters behind their backs without knowing that we are not as different as we may think. We all want LOVE and were built good at the core, our experiences are different throughout our journey but we can relate in some form. Feel your pain as if it is your own. Journeys are meant to be experienced, the ups, the downs, and the indifferent. Sisters are birthed through the same parent (s), they have a genetic connection that extends beyond the normal encounter.

Not only do birth sisters form these relationships but female friends and encounter can be so valuable, to have someone to speak to honestly and openly with no judgement is a masterpiece. I remember the little girl who wanted to be on TV, that desire came from my love for talking and attention. Surprise!! Surprise!!

Eye Popping Puzzles

Who's 12?

A great dancer and gay?

Who's 18 and in front of men don't know what to say?

Who's skinny but short and considered a dork?

Who's the Best Rapper Alive?

The best lyricist?

The youngest entrepreneur?

The inventor of drugs?

The first to buy?

The first to sell?

Shorter than my thigh

No lie

Eye Popping Puzzles I can't solve

I guess we'll have to get God involved

The True Baddest Chick

The True Baddest Chick
Her name is Bri

At one point, I thought it was me

With one hug, life doesn't seem as bad
With one kiss, with God I'm not mad
but
24/7, she's not with me

My uncomfortable position, I'm focused on a mission

Left my Sister, A missing

The Sister who she loves so much, I just want to feel her touch

Sooner than Later

I'll be able to give her the World

Because She's My World

A world wind, This World Is

But when the World ends I'll be proud of what she's done

We'll be on a never ending journey and our friendship has just begun

Ant

advanced natural talent
they show them on Americas Got Talent

such a variety of Talent There
Naturally they were given gifts

They use to uplift
some fall in a drift

of sleep, they are distant
away, they couldn't provide

they had to be the best-which left
the true purpose of the gift
Adrift

On an island or a peninsula of some kind
Your talent was one of a kind
But they'd rather settle in line

Out of line they were
So I gave them the cure

A new lane
A new road, new taxes, new toll
Marshay's stroll

Couldn't Die

Curious and Young
Ms. Carter son
Grabbed a gun
Loud music, he rapped
Didn't know he was strapped

So he continued to rap
Then snap, an accident had occurred
While he was searching for a cure
police came, stuck he couldn't blame

No one but himself
God spoke to him
Told him to go to the living room
Police burst in
In the hospital, a young child cried for help

Young and curious
An MC he was ready to be
But it almost ended, this moment was not splendid
But at 17, his proudest moment of money he could spend
it
To his mother every dime was given

Now therefore God kept him for Living

The Best Rapper Alive
Lil Wayne, Thank God he's still alive

Picasso

a painting some may see
Underneath, I see his Life and how he'd be
the emotion it conveys
Less words is more beautiful to portray
I like them all
Each has its own traits
When I look at it, I see it's face
It has no race
I can see it for who it truly is
With no stereotypes, pre-judgment there
I am able to enjoy beautiful art
Like Mozart
Life imitates Art
Or Art imitates Life
art is a rare form
Life is one's own journey
His/her Life Battle
Picasso Creation
Collazo Invitation
To a Harry Potter situation

Trapped In The Closet

Trapped In the closet

More like open to the bed
Each one of you, could have been dead
Just for a pleasurable moment, you'd risk your life instead
Sylvester was angry when a man answered the phone
Imagine how the pastor felt when he walked into his home
He thought he had his wife to himself, all alone
See that's the mindset of a man, that's grown
But messing with Chuck that's wrong
Preaching against homosexuality
But he didn't face his own reality
A midget thought his wife was pregnant
Found out, he was negligent
But the nosy neighbor must have never experienced life
cause she's so busy in everyone else's
This story becomes combined when they found out everyone
got caught up in mankind
The beauty of a woman's behind
They told their friends to get in Line

Territory

Claim a territory
No terrorists allow
It's our nation, we'll go wild

To claim one place as your home

You got to be careful when you enter someone's zone
because they feel they own
An honor of confidence, their prone to receive
They never want to leave

Divided, they leave the world
United we aren't but are supposed to be

The United States of America
WE
put each branch on a different tree
each root indebted into the ground a different fruit grows around

Differences go all around

Four Voices

The pain inflicted again and again
My inner voice keeps telling me to do it
Why I hear someone yelling you can't

Then I hear my other half saying not like this
But they just don't understand the pain I've endured
And I'm sure they'll say
There's so much more in store

But I'm sick of hearing it
I'm ready to close the door
Then I hear another voice speak to me
This one is unfamiliar but I'm ready to see

My name is God
Your journey has just begun
Put down the gun!!

City

DMV- Da Main Village

Filled with a variety of people, a beautiful image
Money, clothes, shoes and Go-Go was important for enjoyment in life

Considered one, they were not divided by a knife

DMV- Dangerously More Vicious
Plenty of young children filled with ambition
who settled for normal, didn't hit their mission
Let the Fears of the world squeeze them into intermission, an uncomfortable position

DMV- Defining My Vision

Definition of me, I will finally let the World See
As I travel across the world seas, the world will find their own definition of me

DMV- My City!

Lesson 7: Childlike Tales

As a child, we live without question, very curious minds that have many questions. We often receive false perceptions and/or covered up answers to our pondering thoughts. Questions like "Where does babies come from?" or "Why is my skin this color and daddy's is different?" We often tell kids something funny like birds, bring the babies to mommy and she takes care of them like your or we say something like God gave mommy a present. We love feeling like kids of unaware of the harsh world we live in selling them fairytale stories such as Cinderella, Snow White, Elsa and Anna, Ariel. Nothing is wrong with protecting a child from adult content or things that could be potentially harmful. Be sure to grow with them as their minds grow, be open and honest and give realistic information the older they get so the world doesn't be the first to teach them.

Allow them to be children when necessary, live without worries and bills. How many of us would love to go back to the time when we had no bills?? Teach them to handle their responsibilities and make mature, adult decisions.

Wild Child

Wild child, irrational behavior, always yelling to their parents 'I'll see you later"

Clothes ripped up in certain places, makeup filled all over their faces

No problems do they fear to face

Every mistake they leave a trace, if you know your child you can see it on their face

Thongs, lingerie with lace, the problem is at the base

Deeply invest to deeply progress

Emotionally they have a disconnect, so their bodies they feel they have to sell it

Male may sell drugs because at home, they receive no love

Some may have everything but the money to them is everything

Encourage them to treat their lives as Something

Wild Child, is a cry for help

Listen, next time they yelp

Step Child

Once knew a man, did everything for his wife's child he can

Step Child, he was

But his love wasn't a step down from Larry's own four kids

This man was blessed with a strong head, an ability to Love, no matter the circumstances

Forgiveness, he had

Never let a situation get him too mad

Sometimes I wish he was my dad

Worked three jobs with three cars and one wonderful home

Which was fit for a King's Throne

Wife, treat a King like he deserves

his Queen, that spot is reserved

Dead

I don't understand, I understand what they say

Not confused, I still Live everyday

Death, what happens to me cause' I could never see the death of Me

My passion and love dead, it never dies

always awake even before I open my eyes

when someone dies, I never quite realize

the impact to me it feels like they are taking a nap

Detrimental
Emotional
Amazed at Death

I know it feels like they left but in heaven they are

Still confused, what happen to the spirit, this Mind

It will no longer Be Mine

Castings

Cast me in movie
It will gain if I sang
The audition is close
I sit chewing on my toast
Now a stain on my clothes
This boy sags his pants

We're SAVING THE LAST DANCE

Against all Odds

against all odds I saw Wale
In Anne Arundel mills, frozen, I had so much to say

So I text Nay
My mother next

Wale looked smaller in person, two body guards
He was still a normal person

Stepped in and stepped out
I was ready to leave out

of the store but I found my dress to wear to the CTMD tour

with Tyga, Mindless Behavior and Twist and more

These little boys my sister would adore

Against all odds, oddly no one walked up to him
Maybe they were as shocked as I am

Sunoco

Stop blocking my sunlight

Cast a spell in the night light

Didn't u just say God was going to make sure everything was alright

But you still say your struggling, maybe it's because what you thought, wasn't,

Maybe because what you I was, really wasn't

Never realizing who you truly are

Never apologizing for any of your mistakes thus far

Always worried about what somebody is and can't do
Who they are, can affect you

but you won't let you get out of the way
Allow Life to teach you to do things in a better way

Satisfy U No One gets you into Heaven, Only God Can

WORST

Have you ever noticed that your worst feature can become your best asset?

The reason being is because if you didn't have it, you wouldn't add that

God realizes that the biggest turmoil in your life becomes the reason your successful

Every insecurity that you overcome will one day be the reason your able to have fun

At the end of life's battle, you won

Have you noticed how the same person who had you smiling could be the person to cause you to cry?

Have you ever wondered why?

Maybe because after every situation, you look up in the Sky

Thank God

Your able to fly

Worst way sometimes turns out to be the best Travel

but you'd rather ignore bridges when they build new levels and new heights

Your skyrocketing through LIFE

FALSE PROPHECY

Angels, r talking to u, yea right?
You are crazy, u needed someone to satisfy u at night
So u stole a Taurus girl made her fight for the right to sleep
comfortable at night

All because u needed someone to comfort u at night
Raped her but couldn't take away her light

with the power of God, she was able to ignite

First baby at 14, Little girl, she was just a teen
With all my power, I will form a team
A battle against u and every raper (kidnapper)
IT WOULD SEEM

Your life ruined, it's a DREAM

What u took from her, shell never get back
For that reason, I hope they break u back
You should be raped of your life and never to get it back
End up in hell, jail to you is just a snack

Wait until the queen react
The way I respond will last your whole life, a marathon
In the backyard, a tent she was forced to live in
I'll be the force that reckoned

Planned it perfectly, you thought, how this little girl was caught
Even got pass the court bus couldn't pass my court

Battle me on the football field, I turn your head until a football drill

This is LIFE, this is real

your false imagination
how you were god's reincarnation

but now you're
under the power of the nation, incarcerated
yes, you are

you did nothing but formed a Superstar

angels spoke to her the whole time, god protected her the whole time

Now all you have is jail

Prepared

I always got my rack
I double pack
If you ever need anything, I got your back
Like Tia and Tamera, we were twins
everybody in school knew we were best friends

But it came to a halt, an End
All because of a man our relationship started to descend
Our own mothers wanted us to make amends
But as stubborn as you are

I'll see death before I receive an apology
It wasn't my fault your man based everything off astrology
You should have saw the signs when he kept mentioning my signs

Saying God was sending him the signs
That I was that special type, that kind
A boy wouldn't mind to spend the rest of his life with
Little did you notice
I was your friend not Otis
anything he said we had was bogus
But your discretionary skills were atrocious
Diss your sister for a man

Who liked me but I couldn't stand the sight to see
I only focused on the love I had for you
This is what love could do
Break U

You weren't prepared for a relationship
It takes smart head to take care of a relationship

Module 8: Worst Behavior

Men will treat you at the level of your self-esteem, please don't be a foot stool that he steps on to reach the next level while you are still down but instead be an elevator that could take him to the next level while going to the next level with him. Be a lady and handle yourself with class, it is never okay to degrade your mind, body, spirit and/or soul. Learn to evolve as technology has, constantly growing and evolving, getting better each time. It is okay to have fun, let loose and LIVE. Dive into your next best thing after your storm. It's okay to fall, just remember to get back up after whatever has tried to knock you down. WE all will suffer at some point, lose at some point and fight to regain. You have everything in you to succeed.

"The sky is not the limit, it is just the view," a line that is in one of my poems. This line means just because the sky is what you can see, does not mean it is as far as you can go. Just because you can't see it, doesn't mean it cannot possibly happen. Have faith that your goals are obtainable. Use what I would call your "GOOD BRAIN" in every move you make, think twice before making life changing decisions and be true to who you are.

Lives Here

One place I visited for half my life, the other the same
Temple Hills, I am from
Raised, I overcome
Living, I just begun

Sick of the confusion, don't live on an old delusion
Live Here, Live Where
I didn't live here nor there

School begun at 7:45, my school didn't begin till I was alive
Till I wave the momentous of yesterday, goodbye
My thoughts were always above the sky

I fly- No Permanent Home
No place to call my own
Secluded, Deluded
I didn't know you could do it
Intrude it, that's what I felt I did
a place to lay me head
Have I found my home?
Not yet but I will
The moment I am able to stand still

Mood Change

Mood Changed
With your presence, my thoughts were rearranged
You called me insane, all I wanted to do was sang
Happily, I listened to Chrisette
When u came in, I felt fat, bloated and loaded
My heart you can't decode it
The message, I already told it
Everything I said, you'd hold it
Everything I did, you'd ignore but the worst side of me you must adore
Cause you bust down the door
Every time, I held back
To you, I noticed, everything you'd lack and I stack it in your head
So you'd irritate me, make me dread
This is what you said
I did but I really didn't
My mood changed, with your presence
My thoughts became deranged, rearranged
This, I know but Anything else, you can't convince me

Heart Definition

When I sat in the room and I cried, my emotions in front of God
I could not hide

That part of me of the both of you, died
I lied

but it was a dream to be opposite of you both

Cause u rode on the coast, not being horrible but never too good, you thought you did everything you should

The moment my heart burst, you would

Understand, why I felt the way I DID

I WAS NOTHING BUT A CHILD, A KID WHEN I FACED THE DIFFICULTIES OF ADULTS

WITH MY EMOTIONS, I FOUGHT
The moment when I became a woman

Officially to me at age 16, you couldn't see me past a teen

But my attitude is my fault, I allowed you to cause the pain
I fought and I was caught, Confused and Angry

My Heart Definition was the Love I was Missing

Hate Pink or Loved Blue

Pink or Blue

Which one are you?
My fave was dresses, heels and jewelry
Wore pink a lot but I hate pink, right?
Girly, they would call me but my favorite color was blue
I'd rather clean the cook

Which one are you?
Blue, they would buy you and pink for me
all they based it on was the outer appearance, you see
Pink or Blue, at a baby shower, one of these colors we must choose
To tell the difference one of these colors we must use
But what about you?

Which one are you?

Are you super smart or definitely dumb?
Are you boring or do you like to have fun?
Would you rather a daughter or a son?
Do you love to sit down or run?
Your journey has just begun!!

Prodigal daughter or **Prodigal** son

We won
I am a combination of both
A Contradiction, I boast

BET

B-E-T--Black Entertainment Television

Yes, I watch you, I'm so blessed and thankful for things you do

No other has acquired, the ability to inspire
I wish I can acquire with great artistry, I do admire

The ability to inspire

With great artistry, I can't deny (a)

B-E-T, created with a purpose If you Be (e) T, you be with me
Weird, they may call u but I call u unique
The best we can be- if we see

They may call you a freak or a geek but I call them weak

B-E-T: bet they wouldn't know how it is to be a queen
When u reign with God, sometimes it may not seem
Cause' your pain can make em' gleam
but in the end, it's a Dream

Bodacious, Vivacious, Temptations

True Beauty- in the talent, we behold, listening to what we were told, not going down the wrong road

Be Bold

Bodacious, Vivacious, Temptations

Pregnant with a Spiritual Birth

In church you were raising your hand

And clapping when they talked about a trifling man suddenly you were pregnant with a spiritual birth but the baby must have burst

Cause for a minute

The same way you were hollering and ranting
How you'd never let a man in, you became his demand in

and kept on denying

You were lying but you couldn't understand why I made your problems mine because you couldn't see the part of me that was kind

I might fuss and whine but u could have so many men in line
That's my reason, some are there for a season but u made it a Lifetime
Please don't have your life end up on Life time

Not trying to down, not trying to diss, I hope you would finally listen to this

"When a man findeth' a wife, he findeth' a good thing"

Don't feel as though you must settle for less, it doesn't have to be a mess, he doesn't have to be a pest

The devil messes with your mind cause for that, he couldn't mess with mine

HARD LIVING LIFE

There is so much in my life-that I cannot realize

What I'd did long time ago? Glad u didn't know

Sorry if I broke some hearts, I am just broken heart

Hard Living Life- I was a horrible wife

Messed up both of our lives

I'm so glad you're still alive

I'm so glad you're still alive

When he pulled out that knife, that night

Could have taken out your eye, all because I chose to be sexually

Connected to a married man and worse part about it- I'm a married woman

Hard living Life - Hard Living Life - Hard

I caused my own difficulties trying to blame everything on you

Now-------------What am I going to do?

I am so confused----- How can I make it up to u?

You probably don't want to see my face- Baby

But I luv ya, just in case ya' was skeptical

Sorry for going that low-------------I promise I'm not a hoe

But my life has been hard----------------Hard Living life

Didn't mean to make life living hard

Didn't mean---

Failure is not fatal but failure to change maybe

I don't want to take the chance so I'm a lady

I keep my privacy, just like T.I. says privately

and anyone who knows me- knows I am the honesty

You can always be honest with me

To get through life you should be truthful or you'll be regretful

Sorry to Impose

I decided to impose on your brain
And I know u probably thinking I'm insane
But to train
I must understand the effect
And realize the neglect
I decided to impose on your brain
A headache has formed as I enter
In rare form I begin to cement ya
But as I'm building your foundation
I hit a hard rock
For some reason I had to stop
There was something that made me drop and almost fall out
But I grasped on to that little piece of you that didn't have doubt
I whispered to that portion of you
Failure, no more will do

I grabbed the bolt I saw connected to the screw that was near
I knew something was off in your head but as I grabbed the bolt
It was heavy to bare
I begin to look within it, STARE!!
And I discovered something hidden that no one else knew,
you were a female before you turned into a dude
And you've created a lie to tell your wife
She didn't realize, she was happy with her life
No wonder you walked with your head down
And talked in shame
You were a grown man, playing a game
That female that you tried to make leave, never left
It was just a bolt that wasn't connected to a screw
That had you all confused But now What shall you do?

#BLACKBOYS

It's unfair to say the least, how they can unleash the beast
and with a simple release; they value your life the least

So easy just to see you lay, lifeless and say

that the color of your beautiful brown skin is not what
made them pull the trigger and End

Oh No, it's something you did- I think being black, there's
a target on your head and for some odd

reason they don't tread lightly, maybe they think they can
repeat the past with no consequences,

they still walk the streets freely but there's one man above
all who doesn't lie in a casket

His name is God and skin color to him is not a factor in
your quality of life

They fear you most and let me tell you why

Your strength is unbearable so they'd rather see you die

They are not thinking about how one day, you could be the
same very man to who save their life or

even introduces them to their next wife, they don't fret to
think about your kids or lives you will lead

but chance is you're within reach of perfect and their fear causes them to pull the trigger as your hands are raised

All of a sudden, the bullet graze(s) right through your heart and a life full of golden treasure, they watch drop

As your heart stops, theirs begins to beat

And as a man they finally feel the strength to stand on their feet

Like Jesus is to God

Like Jesus is to God

I wish Your Love could go that far
my fallen star

I had my mind convinced to give you a try
but all I've done during this time was cry

pain causes me to write, like glasses does a blind man his sight

I've given up my fight

one day I see you learning that fear is not funny

when the thing you fear most, faces you and chases you

don't take that last line as a threat but a promise that a lesson will be learned

no value of cash can replace me or be earned

unconditional love, that's all I ask for
you would hate me if I asked more

Precious

Raped constantly all your life
Put through life's greatest strife
The man you're supposed to call your 'Daddy"
The woman whose supposed to be your mom
Has been alarmed
Of this behavior that occurred
In her eyes, she seen it but let it be blurred
Impregnating you with two kids
Both who he knew was his
One being born with a disorder
Of this pain, it brought her
She never cared if you ever learned
The inside of her was burned
Not only did she force you to cook
But her nasty private you had to look
You as a child, your innocence was took
Never to be returned but always overlooked
God sent a miracle into your life
Like a stab sent through a knife
A teacher to help you have strength to move on
Allowing you to mourn
Of your pain, she was not warned
When she returned a message
You let her know of their damage

With class mates their as your support
Revenge was not your nearest resort
Letting you know of a maybe to a deadly disease
Of your youngest child, you worried of his needs
When tested through doctors, your intimate relationship
with your child was torn
This disease you now carried was worn
Aids was no aid at any age
Being 16 made it ten times worst, we understand your rage
But you carried yourself, unhappy of whom you are
Insecure, never knowing you were a star
Dreaming of being bigger than you knew you were
It relation to your size, it has a cure
Beautiful
Smart
Successful

Module 9: Inside of Me

I have always been misunderstood, people have viewed me differently than I found myself. Inside of you I see a fighter, a warrior, a survivor, a thriver and a goal getter. You are not who you previously were, you have failed, made mistakes and been imperfect but life is a learning journey. Bring out the inner you through prayer, self-examination and self-acceptance. Birth the baby in your womb, you have carried this baby for nine plus months and she has come full term, it is time for her to come out. Birth her, then give her the tools to grow, live and develop to birth and raise a baby of her own. God is proud of the work you have done. He appreciates you!!

Do YOU? Inside of you is the ability to navigate through life, push past the hurt and whether the storm.

Forget THAT Fast

Buy you a car and a new pair of shoes
Does everything to be your dude

Did you forget that fast that it never did last or do you call that forgiving?
I know women who keep sinning

Who know they are wrong but the feeling is so strong
He is not going to make it last, no matter how much you try

He'll always go to the other side
You think you have solved the puzzle, have the key to his heart but you two couldn't be farther apart

If only you knew the truth
There's a statement that says "you remember what you want"

And as women, that's what we do
We tend to forget the truth

When honestly he's been telling you
The entire time, where you belong in his life and what he's willing to do

But you confuse Pain with Love
and that's just you

Play-DOH

I loved you like I knew how

You tricked me into believing you loved me back

When truly you'd play behind my back

Play-DOH

You must be a kid

'I Do'

Cause I don't know you
So why you standing so close
You right up under my nose
Don't bring me no flowers, no chocolate or gold cause
We ain't friends- I don't like you like that I thought I did
I thought I'd marry you and have a kid
My heart is broken
You can move on
My heart so torn, scorn and worn
Hey- I do
Ain't messing with you
Faking like you a prince charming
Coming to give the princess her kiss
So, she could get out of this
But situations got worse
You made an outburst
She didn't like that
When I leave out the door
Don't worry or fret
My # better not be called
Cause I promise yours won't

My Choice

Ain't going stop... no, no, no
Pain and sorrow ain't in control
I'm going to show you how to roll
Not the past that predicts my future
Cause I could have been an abuser
User and a loser
But I choose not to lose, never used and won't abuse
It ain't in me no, no
I can't let it stop me
Won't let them drop me
I am destined to be
My fate is my decision, it's up to me
I ain't going stop no
It's my choose to choose
Not to use abuse or lose
I am Greater
My faith is the greatest

Left Eye

It was my left eye
Through I could see so far
Within I could see a star

It was my Left Eye
It blinked the most
It would tear the fastest

With my Left Eye, I saw hope
With my Left Eye, I saw change
From that Left Eye, life was rearranged

The left eye represented my pain
It gave me my strength
I was not in need of him
Lopes was name, Lisa was it too and I knew Lopes meant strength and change
For life from now on, I would see through that Left Eye
My Left Eye showed me struggles are preparation for what's yet to come
I know my left Eye was change
My goal is to move forward
Never looking back

You were there but not here

You were always in my life
There through each minute of strife

But did you help me, did you care?

I could not find you anywhere

You were in my life but were you there?

Through each moment I've cried
Through each tear I've shed

My love was always ahead

I've known you were in my life but you were not there

I had to be strong, I had to stand on my own

You did not have my back

You did not protect me
You did not back me up
You did not obey my needs

Did you care if I would succeed?

I gave you all my heart, I prayed all night to my Lord

God spoke with me and said I am Here

I felt God and he was all I needed So I thank you

My Awardee

Worthy of being acknowledged

Fighting through a war determined to make it out

Learning that situations of results include doubt, when you receive it you should scream

You should shout!

It's your time to be acknowledged, your time to shine

You don't have to wait in line

Patience is key is what they state to me

They say our generation has none

Patience, they want it now

Been in the business at least 20 years

Walked with a good heart, now she's running with success

Monique is my winner, she is the best

Peace

This is peace
This is Love
This is me

Protection, Security
Dedication, Dignity

Relaxation is my sensation. I want peace
Don't like arguing, fussing or fighting,
My maturity level has come to a rise
Float like a butterfly, sting like a bee
Quotations by Muhammad but not me
Stand up and Raise your hands
Take, take a stand!!
For what you believe in Peace
It can come true, it's possible

This is Peace

This is hope

This is love

This is me

Peace

Module 10: My Heart Cries

My heart cries for the black boy afraid to admit he was touched. My heart cries for the black mother whose son life was snatched by the hand of the police. My heart cries for the brothers, sisters, aunts and cousins of these victims. My heart cries for my nation that allowed Donald Trump to make it this far in the presidential campaign. Hillary is our next president and I am so proud to say that she is a woman. My heart cries for the children who won't understand their worth because their community hasn't taught them their value. They need to be encouraged, uplifted and inspired for them to be who they are designed to. My heart cries for the gorgeous dark skinned girl who cannot see the beauty that she carries.

My heart cries for those who allow color to determine their value of another human being on earth. Help as many people in the world as you can, no matter what they do with your help, you will be blessed for helping. Be present and alert, learn new things, help new people and smile as often as possible.

There was no ending to the DRAMA

The drama would not end
It acted as my friend

I had my mother with no dad
And shared my room with three brothers I had

I had 12 siblings and I was the oldest
I was always the boldest

I had to stay strong for my mother would fault as wrong
I had to be so bold with no blankets at night for her to hold when it was cold

The would not end
School was curved and it had to bend or soon my life would come to an end
I wanted to succeed

My mother cared in deed but with twelve siblings it was hard for the cash
For that special moment, would last

I had to work, work, and work
No time to play or jerk

Time had passed
Memories would last of all the days I wondered
After all the times, I was coming
I kept wondering

When will there be an ending to the drama

No Trespassing!

You must start here

End there

Never crossing the line- Never being behind

Don't put one foot on the other side

Be ready to go for the ride

Knowing your limits

Never exceeding them

Shows your courage, honesty, and integrity

Trespassers have consequences

Beyond the imagination

Destroying the nation

Giving statistics so high

And limits that reach the sky

Try, Try, Try

Wanting to do more than you can

Wanting to do more than you can

Stuck in a problem that's so deep

It's like a high mountain that's too steep
Being confused, having no one to tell it all

At the end of the day, you feel as though you'll fall

You have plenty of struggles, plenty of battles to fight

You are fighting in the day, even the night

You want to work harder, you feel as though you can

The problem may only subdue

The struggle is bigger than you

Wanting to do more than you can

Loving em' all, not wanting no one to struggle or fall

Just keep going - God is answering the call

Trees

Trees they stand mighty and bold
Being strengthened through the cold
Standing tall nothing to hold
Providing the oxygen for us all
Giving us a breeze before the sun falls
Never being taken down, living still with a crown
Trees hold on to their roots
Letting many leaves fall
Broadcasting over a long range
Trees are powerful in so many ways
All of them couldn't be stated in this poem I made
Through trees we see more clearly
We see everything from on top
Trees have feelings, they have a heart
Nothing has to pass by or say 'hi'
Trees never bow goodbye
Trees are themselves
They have a personality
My tree is a tree that we all see

My Frenemies

I don't care if you dislike me

Others do, too

I only love you

But my liking of you is optional

State lies mix with the truth

Hate a child of God and she'll love you in return

Claim you have a struggle, you are blindsided to the truth

I am honestly inclined and know what to do

You don't take care of me like you think you do

You are around me as the person who carried me for nine months

Our relationship has suffered for years, and finally it's your chance to be here

Be honest with yourself

Live your truths

Because lies are not becoming of you

Tax Money

Tax Money

Without it

I'm bitter, angry and filled with frustration pointed right toward you and you and you

Only because truthfully who deserves the blame is the unfathomable

My instigator, my feeder, my girlfriend

I use my personal lies towards destination

Never reaching my goal, she was stronger I should have known

Still going to receive it so why make her suffer while I

Bitter makes me sour but I'm so sweet

Nothing was received, I got my treat

Forgiveness

Forgiveness is an inner peace
Given with love like only a niece
Identifying that it's okay, what was done is gone and put away

Never to let the fact go but with happy within in your soul

Forgiveness is accepting the fact that you know
Being able to move on, being able to mourn

Forgiveness is hard to conquer but once learned and once known the strength will come within its own

Having the joy that's not only within but given so near it's like a friend

Receiving the love, giving it, too
The only block between it is you

So, please don't stand in the way, move inside and let forgiveness ride

For I will forgive all who is deserving and all who are not
I will have an inner peace

Forgiveness I speak Forgiveness

Great Grandma Claudette

God gives us the serenity to keep what can't be changed and courage to change what can't be kept and strength to know the difference

The brightest personality mixed with the warmest smile

Greeting us with your presence for awhile

You were never afraid to hide what was on your mind

You would always stand there, and look them in their eyes with pride

As you would say 'no one was quite as pretty as you'

I learned to know this statement was true

You had the wildest comments like no one I knew
You would say 'Hot Dog' AND 'Ding' Ding' Ding'

Potato Salad being your best dish

Green being the color of envy

It was your favorite, it deserved an Emmy

Dancing being such a unique technique

Your moves is what everybody seeks

One thing you were…NEVER weak

Rainbow

At the end of the road there is a rainbow

Trials and Tribulations

Stormy Situations

Only make me stronger

No regrets No longer

Cause I see my golden, my golden gate, await my day

Cause I have faith, at the end of the road there is a Rainbow

Out of everything we been through, I tried to keep the line open

Tried to communicate but I guess I tried too late

As long as my lord knows

At-the-end-of the-road-there-is-a

RAINBOW

The Heart Should be as Light as a Feather

When weighed on a scale and compared

They should be even, they should balance out because if u truly have loved like u should and cared like u stated

Your heart would be elated and have no pounds of stress

Cause you gave God your best

If u had no last worries or desperate despair

Then a true love was always there

I know feathers are soft but with that your heart as compassionate as it should be

Soft and Carefree

Release all that you were

God being in control, with him at the master that knows

The heart should be as light as a feather

Love like only you can

Feathery, softly and light and beautiful in sight,

Your heart should be, too

Filled with joy, not a void

Check with God to see if your heart is as light as it should be or does it have some fixing concerns

See sometimes we blame too much and put ourselves in deeper struggles than God has in store

        We dig deeper holes into the ground

Module 11: Never Ending

Life is a never-ending journey, even when it ends here on Earth. It is a grand experience that not everyone is rewarded. Relationships should be treated as such, NEVER Ending. When God puts two people together, it will require a lot of work, time and patience but in the end, it will all be worth it. I need you to push past what you were taught were the boundaries set and change lives in a manner, others event. God can do the Impossible, believe that his miraculous powers are all over your life and moving on the inside of you.

<u>Window Seat</u>

The window seat is where we meet

I face you as you face me

I view your traits as you view my characteristics

I see your mannerism as you see mine

We view each situation in its own kind

No one's beside me, so the only opinion that counts is mine

It feels as though this ride is not empty or is not alone even though there's no one riding along

I look at you and suddenly feel filled

My Window Seat

Where visions meet

Jump Up In the Air and Stay There

Sometimes I just want to jump up in the air and stay there
The momentous feeling that I receive
Makes me never want to leave
In this place, I don't grieve
It's a breath of fresh air
Intoxicating as inhale it in, I realize this place is my new best friend
It's a place that can't be seen through a telescope
It's a place of growth where I cope
Jump up in the air and stay there
We all want this opportunity
We all need this chance but only few are awarded it and only little enhance
This is my chance
Once I jump in the air
I will Stay There

That Thing, That Thang

That thing has you addicted to drugs
that thang is your search for love

That thing has you posing as a man, that thing is the touch
of his hand
That thing has you stripping at Black Diamonds
That Thang is him breaking your hymen

That thing has your smoking weed
That thang is the influence and the hustler's greed

That thing, that thang cane to kill, steal and destroy
Will you get caught in a trap or finish every lap?

I grab you who is addicted to drugs and I give you love
I grab you posing as a man, I grab your hand

I tell you to release the fear
God is here

I grab you stripping at Black Diamonds
Now you're smiling

I grab you who keeps smoking weed
I take the blunt out of your hand

And show you "I Can"
lead as an example, Barack is just a sample

Three Blind Mice

three Blind Mice
sitting there playing nice
acting like everything's all good
three blind mice
got everyone
going to join the line of lice
not helpful at all, cold as ice
three blind mice
I rarely understand
I know you're blind but you must be deaf, too
because you've never heard the defeat done to you
Defeated you've been and it never ends
We must try and at least be like Stevie Wonder
Wonderful even though he's blind but still on his grind
Three blind mice, they surely cannot last
They are not as great as they believe
Three blind mice, they will not achieve

Module 12: I Envision

I envision a world where we will love purely. I envision a world where our will to help is boundless, we do not have to beg or suffer without the help being accessible and obtainable. I envision a nation where God leads us all in love, we do not judge our brethren but push them to be better. God is not someone we just lean on when we need help but he is the director of our stage play. Our mindsets our not in bondage by past hurts and fears but our challenged to do the unimaginable. I envision our young women representing more than just their bodies as ads to their level of self-esteem. I envision a world where our fathers are no longer a thing of the past but are our protectors, providers and preservers of our families.

I envision fathers being in the household raising children, being husbands to their wives, working and worshipping.

Living On The Verge

I'm Living on The Verge
Never knowing what is heard

Life is a struggle, My life is hard
I been on drugs and Can't Stop
If I fall, I'll drop

I have no one there, nobody who's got my back
So I continue to sit there letting it get slapped

I got a man yes it's true but he's a broke man just like you
He does what he wants; he says I do what I do
He's on the streets still hustling with his crew

I got a crew too, except with us we wear less clothes you may call us hoes
Us women we got to stand strong, we have to live life

No matter if we living wrong
I grew up real fast; life is all about getting that cash
I sit in my normal spot, showing both the front and back
Education that is what is lack

Never got taught from no private school, living a life that was rude and cruel
Having no family, got ghetto little friends
One thing I knew was the struggle never ends

When I look back over all I've done

None of it was even that fun but at the end of the day, I know that I chose

I chose to be still here with these hoes

I could have changed, could have worked a little harder but this here is my running starter

Me starting to write, now this I know I know I can do

Writing about my Dreams, I'm going to make come true

Autobiography:

Marshay Herder is a poet, entrepreneur, blogger and author. She began writing at the tender age of eight. She has journaled her life story on paper from a young age unto now without even knowing that God would one day lead her into publishing a book of poetry titled "The Meaning of My Story." Marshay Herder was an extremely shy, quiet and reserved young woman who is now pushing past boundaries that were set for her. She has always voiced her opinion on certain subjects such as school, moral, faith and her approach to life; often debating with close family and friends on controversial subjects. She is extremely passionate about serving her purpose in life and has been on a journey to help others do the same. Marshay loves working with children, music, fashion and entertainment. Her brand #WithPassion is a spit-fire, fashion, lifestyle and entertainment business with plans on major expansion over the next few years.

"The Meaning of My Story"

This thought-provoking, emotionally charged book entails poetry, written and arranged by Marshay that tells the story of her life including details that others would least expect. Pick up your copy today, available everywhere to purchase. This is just the beginning of her journey, there's so much more in store!!

Visit her website at withpassion.com

Follow @MarshayH on Twitter, Instagram and Periscope

Follow @MarshayModels Entertainment on Facebook and Twitter

Follow @Misfits on Instagram

Follow @Passion2With on Twitter and Instagram

Thank You

Marshay Herder would like to Thank God, first and foremost for being the leader and love of her life. Secondly, I would like to thank my sister Bri'on Herder for being my inspiration to never give up even when trials and tribulations faced me. I would like to thank my grandmothers Yolande Gary and Bobbie Smith for assisting God in raising me, keeping me grounded and focused. I would like to thank my mother Yovon Herder and father Marlow Bush Jr. for being exactly who you are, I love you with everything I am!! Without you, there would be no me!! I would like to thank my cousin Keami for being more like a sister throughout my whole life. I would like to thank all my little cousins, who are more like my own kids (lol), without you all I wouldn't have the drive to go for what God has for me; thank you all A'miyah, Jalan, Landon, Gabby, Savannah, Sasha, Noah and of course my heavenly baby Jayde for uplifting me and encouraging me without trying. I would like to thank my aunts Janay and Shavon Gary for being second mothers. I would like to thank all my family and friends because in some way, some form and some shape you have formed the person that I am today and you are a part of all the stories I tell. I love you all beyond imagine.

I haven't forgotten you Romelo, thank you for the laughter throughout my life. Thank you to my cousin Keon whom I could always have long conversations with and without saying anything at all, we have a bond that is unbreakable. Thank you to Shalanda, my cousin that I always could have a great conversation with and your daughter Christian, whom I could have fun with. Special Thank you to Imani White for being a part of my transformation process and gaining the confidence to release all that I am.

Thank you, Aunt Dana, for your comment stating that I should write a book. I did it and it didn't take me too long!! I would like Thank Tiphani Montgomery for helping me via periscope to realize my purpose, at least for this moment in time. I would like thank Tressa "Azarel" Smallwood for allowing me the opportunity to work with you, learn from you and for recharging my ideas for my book. I would like thank Prophetess Valerie Moore who has encouraged and uplifted me to have this baby, which is my book via periscope. To all of my family and friends: Thank you and I love you beyond imagine. I would like to thank everyone I've ever encountered in life. To God be the Glory, without you father, I am nothing and it is you who has given me life to write, and publish these words that prayerfully change lives positively.

To everyone reading this book, thank you for believing in what God has placed inside of me to enough to purchase this book, I love and appreciate you!!

www.ingramcontent.com/pod-product-compliance
Lightning Source LLC
Chambersburg PA
CBHW060757050426
42449CB00008B/1433